new zealand
from the air

new zealand from the air

TEXT BY
John Gauldie

PHOTOGRAPHY BY
Lloyd Homer

REED

Published by Reed Books, a division of Reed Publishing (NZ) Ltd,
39 Rawene Rd, Birkenhead, Auckland. Website www.reed.co.nz.
Associated companies, branches and representatives throughout the world.

Established in 1907, Reed Publishing (NZ) Ltd
is New Zealand's largest book publisher, with over 300 titles in print.
For details on all these books visit our website:
www.reed.co.nz

This book is copyright. Except for the purpose of fair reviewing, no part of this publication may be reproduced or transmitted in any form or by any means, electronic or mechanical, including photocopying, recording, or any information storage and retrieval system, without permission in writing from the publisher. Infringers of copyright render themselves liable to prosecution.

North Island (sea) cover ISBN 0 7900 0765 7
South Island (mountain) cover ISBN 0 7900 0745 2

© 2000

The author and photographer assert their moral rights in the work.
All photographs by Lloyd Homer except pages 32/33, 107, 149 bottom,
151 top and bottom (Holger Leue) and page 22 top (Bob McCree).

Cover designed by Sunny H. Yang
Text designed by Graeme Leather

First published 2000

Printed in China

The Last Country on Earth

A mammoth volcanic eruption hurled pumice, ash and rocks high into the earth's atmosphere. Collapsing under its own weight, the cloud of debris burst outwards over the land, smothering all in its path within a 90-kilometre radius. Ancient forests were flattened, animals annihilated. It was one of the greatest natural disasters since the beginning of human history.

But no one witnessed it, and the volcano had no name. It rose up from a prehistoric landmass the size of Italy or Japan, beyond the edge of the known world.

The human zeal for exploration and discovery had long since led to the colonisation of every continent except Antarctica, and the world's great civilisations had arisen thousands of years before. But of this distant land, people remained ignorant. Then, following the cataclysmic explosion, debris in the upper atmosphere spread around the world, colouring sunsets and sunrises, from the shrinking Roman empire to the golden Mayan temples. The citizens of these civilisations must have looked at the fiery skies in wonder for without realising it, they were witnesses to the distant event. A land yet to be walked by humans had made its international debut, announcing its presence to the world, the last country on earth.

So, at any rate, goes the popular tale, but recent studies have upset such romantic notions. The sky is supposed to have glowed red over those far-off cities in AD 186, but tree-ring sequencing now indicates the eruption — the enormity of which is not in doubt — took place some 40 years later, in about AD 230, and there appears to be no record in the histories of the world of anything untoward at that time.

Perhaps scientific evidence should not be allowed to spoil a good story. Be that as it may, stories aplenty were soon to be told of the land beyond the edge, for within less than a thousand years people would set foot there. It would become known variously as Aotearoa, Statenland, Nieuw Zeeland and, most recently, New Zealand. Yet by the time it became a country for humans, it was already a land with a long and unique history.

From Gondwanaland, the ancient supercontinent from which many of the world's landmasses are derived, a small strip broke free about 80 million years ago. Mountainous and thickly forested, this breakaway fragment would, over an age of isolation, become shaped into the islands of New Zealand.

Situated on a volatile spot straddling two of the earth's tectonic plates, the land twisted and turned on itself. It was rent asunder by earthquakes and regurgitated by volcanoes. It became buried under fresh deposits, its mountains were shattered into rubble and its plains sank beneath the waves.

Around the coast enormous marine reptiles, such as the mosasaur, dominated the undersea world. Prehistoric turtles and fish swam in the warm waters. On the mountain slopes dinosaurs thrived in the bush, until their world-wide extinction 65 million years ago opened the way for other creatures. The birds that had lived alongside the dinosaurs now had the island to themselves. They were to prosper until modern times, lords of their isolated kingdom.

The birds enjoyed an avian paradise. There were neither mammals nor snakes to fear, food was abundant, and the climate was mild. In the absence of predators waiting to pounce on them, many birds took the opportunity to make their homes on the ground. For these, wings and bulky flight muscles became unnecessary accoutrements.

Among the ranks of this feathered but flightless fraternity, picking its way across the forest floor beneath the branches, was one of the oldest inhabitants of the land — a bird unlike any other. Its evolutionary origins are shrouded in uncertainty, but it is possible the kiwi — or at least the ancestor of the bird we know by that name today — was already to be found among the ferns and tree roots when the land for which it was destined to become an emblem split from Gondwana. If so, it was one of the denizens that truly belonged, and an appropriate choice for human adoption millions of years hence.

The kiwi was a reclusive creature, coming out only at night to hunt for worms, insects and snails. Its eyesight was poor, but keen hearing and nostrils in the end of its long probing beak, with which it sniffed out its subterranean prey, more than compensated. It had no wings, but its strong legs and sharp claws gave it great running speed and a formidable means of defence. An unlikely animal it may have been — in many ways more like a mammal than a bird — but it was equipped to survive.

Moa, like kiwi, were another group of ancient flightless birds. But while the two shared a common, if distant, ancestry, they could scarcely have been more different. Kiwi are about the size of a chicken, while moa ranged in height from half a metre to a giant three metres — the tallest birds ever to walk the earth. Such stupendous size, and the enormous, powerful legs with which they bestrode the landscape, were possible for a bird only once flight had been abandoned. The eleven or so different species of moa were herbivores, browsing shrubs and trees much like deer, bison and antelope in other parts of the world, although they are not thought to have lived in herds (or flocks) like their mammalian counterparts.

Another spectacular bird which did fly, but which has now also, like moa, been lost to time, was the hokioi, a giant eagle. Its three-metre wings made it the largest bird of prey the world has seen, and it was the giant moa's only adversary.

While the bird population flourished, the land continued its radical transformations and contortions, the pattern of destruction and renewal repeating itself over the millennia.

THE LAST COUNTRY ON EARTH

About two million years ago a cycle of ice ages began. Glaciers advanced from the snowfields high in the mountains, gouging deep valleys in what we know today as the Southern Alps, before retreating as temperatures rose once more. Time and again these giant, slow-moving rivers of ice spread across the land, then receded. Following the ice sheets' last retreat, some 10–15,000 years ago, the land had been shaped into the form we see today. The stage was set for the age of *Homo sapiens*.

By now man had spread to most parts of the earth. Only a few corners continued to escape human contact. It fell to explorers from Polynesia to discover the forested land of the south-western Pacific Ocean that had lain in such isolation for so long.

The colonisation of Polynesia itself took place between 3000 and 2000 years ago, and by 1500 years ago settlers had reached distant Hawaii to the north and Rapa Nui — Easter Island — to the east. But the unknown land, with its euphonious kingdom of birds, lay still untouched on the southernmost fringe of the Polynesian world. The explorers who found their way there in about AD 800 came from an island in the heart of the Pacific they called Hawai'iki, which may have been one of the islands near Tahiti.

The Polynesian explorers were navigators supreme. Sailing in giant waka — ocean-going canoes — they used the stars and the direction of the swells to steer a course across vast stretches of empty water. They also searched for signs of land beyond the horizon, such as birds that returned to land after feeding at sea. Clouds, too, could indicate the presence of land, and so it was that the Polynesians who first set eyes on the land far to the south called it Aotearoa — land of the long white cloud.

Discovery of Aotearoa is credited to the explorer Kupe. He voyaged round the North Island and down the west coast of the South Island before returning to his homeland. Kupe shared his discovery with other navigators, who then undertook the same journey.

Thus the settlement of Aotearoa began, the influx continuing until the 14th century, after which contact with the homeland seems to have ceased. The last country on earth to be reached by people was now home to the many tribes of Maori.

The arrival of humans had a dramatic impact, over-exploitation of many species leading to their extinction. Moa and other game birds, used to a largely predator-free existence, were easy meat and soon hunted out of existence (moa were probably extinct by the start of the 17th century). Fur seals were depleted, and the introduced kiore, or Pacific rat, devastated populations of frogs, reptiles and ground-nesting birds. Maori relied increasingly on kai moana — food from the sea — such as fish and shellfish. A sharp increase in the incidence of forest fires resulted in considerable deforestation.

Maori were not only hunters, they were also horticulturists. But most of the plants they brought from Polynesia could not be successfully cultivated because of the cooler climate and shorter growing season. Among the few exceptions were taro, yams and the sweet potato called kumara. To supplement their meagre stock, Maori turned to local wild plants, such as fern root — an important source of carbohydrate when stripped and baked — and various trees, such as tawa, karaka and the cabbage tree.

Intertribal warfare was common among Maori, but off the battlefield they shared a complex and regulated society. Maori art was the most brilliant of all Polynesian art. Lavish meeting houses, canoes, weapons, ornaments and utensils, richly decorated with figures and designs, were carved from native timbers such as kauri and rimu. Ornaments and weapons were fashioned from pounamu, or greenstone (a variety of jade). Cloaks were woven from harakeke, or flax, and decorated with feathers or dogskin. Mats and baskets were also made of flax.

But Maori were not to have Aotearoa to themselves for long. A new wave of settlers was soon gathering on the horizon. European ships first arrived in the Pacific in 1520, when Ferdinand Magellan circumnavigated the globe. The Dutch, based in Indonesia, became a notable power in Southeast Asia and the eastern Pacific Ocean. In 1616 the Dutch explorers Willem Schouten and Jacques Le Maire, who were crossing the Pacific after rounding Cape Horn, encountered a large and well-equipped Polynesian canoe in the open sea north of Tonga. Intrigued by the possibility of finding a large civilisation in the Pacific, the Dutch set to work exploring the uncharted ocean.

Thirty years later, on 13 December 1642, Abel Tasman and the crews of *Heemskerk* and *Zeehaan* sighted the mountains of the South Island. The two ships had stumbled upon the land unknown to Europeans having sailed round Australia and set a course for the Solomon Islands. Making his way up the west coast, Tasman wrote of the inhospitable, jagged terrain.

The two ships rounded the top of the South Island and anchored in what is today known as Golden Bay. Here four Dutch sailors lost their lives when their small boat was intercepted by a canoe of Ngati Tumatakokiri warriors, down from the North Island to fight the local tribes. As more canoes took to the water to engage *Heemskerk* and *Zeehaan*, the Dutch hastily withdrew. They did not attempt to land again. The Dutch East India Company later criticised Tasman for his poor documentation of the land he had come across and for failing to investigate its inhabitants.

Tasman thought he had discovered the west coast of Statenland, a continent believed to stretch across the Pacific Ocean towards South America. At the same time, however, another Dutch navigator, Hendrik Brouwer, was discovering that the east coast did not exist. The East India Company's chart-maker therefore renamed Tasman's find Nieuw Zeeland, after the Dutch province in which the company had one of its business chambers. Similarly, the land to the west — yet to be claimed by the British and called Australia — was named Nieuw Holland after the province in which the company held its principal chamber.

Nieuw Zeeland did not feature again in Dutch plans and caused little interest in the rest of Europe. Its hostile inhabitants and cool climate held scant promise of the valuable tropical spices sought by the Europeans at the time.

More than a hundred years later Captain James Cook set sail from England on *Endeavour* on a voyage round the globe. Over the next ten years he was to visit the Pacific three times, and would eventually die there. Also on board *Endeavour* was the young scientist and explorer Joseph Banks.

THE LAST COUNTRY ON EARTH

Cook had been charged by the British Admiralty to observe the transit of Venus from Tahiti, and to explore and document the lands of the South Pacific, of which so little was known. From Tahiti, *Endeavour* headed south-west to Nieuw Zeeland, her crew sighting the east coast of the North Island on 7 October 1769.

Cook spent more than six months in New Zealand (he anglicised the name conferred by the Dutch), charting the coast while Banks collected botanical specimens, collected Maori artefacts and made hundreds of sketches. The voyage went down in history as one of the most famous and important scientific expeditions ever undertaken.

Following Cook's exploits, it was only a matter of time before others followed. First came whalers and sealers, then missionaries and the earliest settlers. But as the European colonisation of New Zealand began, the prospects for those seeking a new life in a new land weren't always rosy. The long and arduous voyage was the first challenge to be surmounted. Then there was the fight to tame the wilderness and bring it under the plough. As if this wasn't enough, many Maori, by now in possession of muskets, proved fiercely resistant to the invasion of their land. Perhaps greatest of all hardships, however, was the almost complete isolation from the rest of the world. The closest European outpost was the settlement at Port Jackson in New South Wales, over 2000 kilometres away — the distance from London to Istanbul. Despite such wide separation, New Zealand actually fell under New South Wales jurisdiction for a while.

In 1840, New Zealand was annexed by Great Britain and joined the ranks of the British colonies. The Treaty of Waitangi, signed by representatives of the British Crown and many Maori chiefs, sought to enshrine the respective rights and obligations of the Crown and Maori concerning land ownership, and European settlement began in earnest. The bush gave way to pasture for sheep. Forest giants were felled and milled. River deposits and reefs of quartz yielded up gold. Quarries and mines gutted the hillsides for coal. As the timber, gold and coal ran out, forestry, horticulture and dairy farming arose in their place.

Reaping the land of its bounty and then putting it to work devastated the once great forests. Wilderness, untamed since its creation, was transformed by agriculture and construction until only a fraction of the original forest cover remained.

Such devastation was inevitably accompanied by a fresh wave of extinctions, exacerbated by the introduction of new mammalian pests and predators. Rats, cats, dogs, stoats, ferrets, pigs, possums, rabbits and deer all wrought havoc on native wildlife, changing ecosystems and decimating populations. Today, many species that have so far survived the onslaught waver on the edge of extinction. The takahe, an indigo-coloured rail with a large red bill, was believed extinct until the discovery of a small colony in a remote mountain range in 1948. The striking blue-grey kokako, with its rich musical song and bright-blue wattles, is now confined to a handful of sanctuaries. The kakapo, a flightless, nocturnal parrot with an unusual booming call, has become one of the rarest birds in the world. Even the creature with which New Zealanders have come to identify themselves, the kiwi, is under serious threat of extinction.

Today, little more than a thousand years since Kupe first set foot in the last country on earth, it has been irrevocably altered. Fortunately, untouched expanses of natural beauty survive, testimony to the landscape's former glory, and there is a growing awareness of the need to ensure the survival of its remaining indigenous inhabitants. Meanwhile, frequent earthquakes and bouts of volcanic activity serve as a reminder that it is still a volatile and tumultuous place. The pattern of destruction and renewal continues.

In 1995 the world's news media reported on the sudden and unexpected eruption of New Zealand's Mt Ruapehu. Scientists recorded the seismic rumblings, and aeroplanes carrying television cameras circled the cloud of ash and steam. Nearly eighteen centuries after that earlier, gigantic eruption — from the gaping hole that today holds the waters of nearby Lake Taupo — New Zealand once again took its place on the world stage.

Isolated by distance and oceans, prehistoric New Zealand endured while the world around it changed. When Taupo bellowed its presence to the world, the land and its population of birds witnessed an omen of transformation. Whether the world heard the far-off call or not, its navigators and explorers were already rigging their vessels and looking towards the ocean's southernmost horizon.

Northland

At the entrance to Parengarenga Harbour, near North Cape, the blue-green sea rolls against some of the world's purest white silica sand. In the distance Cape Reinga juts out into the turbulent waters that mark the meeting of the Tasman Sea and the Pacific Ocean. Although sometimes visited by locals collecting shellfish, the harbour's beaches are usually deserted. The only footprints in the tide-smoothed sand are made by the measured steps of wading birds.

Cape Reinga is considered the top of New Zealand, although the inaccessible North Cape is at a slightly higher latitude. Cape Reinga is sometimes the scene of fierce subtropical storms. Captain Cook sailed through one as he rounded the cape in 1769, just a few days after beginning his voyage round New Zealand. In the same storm, the French explorer Jean-François Marie de Surville rounded the cape in the opposite direction. The two explorers, possibly passing within calling distance, failed to spot one another through the murk.

Matuopao Island hugs the shore of Cape Maria van Diemen, the North Island's most westerly point. To the south is the long sweep of Ninety-Mile Beach. The Dutch explorer Abel Tasman named the cape as he sailed from New Zealand in 1642 — after Maria, wife of the Dutch East India Company's governor, Antoni van Diemen. Based in Batavia (now Jakarta), van Diemen was the force behind the Dutch exploration of Australia and New Zealand.

Russell, a small town in the Bay of Islands, was New Zealand's first capital. It held this distinction for just nine months in 1840, before handing over to Auckland (which remained the capital until 1865). Russell was originally the site of a Maori settlement called Kororareka, and attracted a large number of ship-deserters and ex-convicts from Australia. In the 1820s and 30s whaling vessels filled the bay, and the village became home to the largest European population in the country. A British officer described the place as 'a vile hole, full of impudent half-drunken people'. Today, the historic township is a centre for big-game fishing and boat tours around the Bay of Islands.

The Bay of Islands is a maritime playground of quiet inlets and undisturbed beaches. Cruising yachts from around the world find anchorage among its 144 islands, while for sports-fishermen it offers the chance to hook a blue marlin or mako shark. Dolphins are year-round visitors in the Bay, as is the subtropical weather, for which the area has been dubbed 'The Winterless North'. The small and scattered population includes a large number of immigrants who have made this secluded corner of the country their home.

One of New Zealand's 13 marine reserves, and rated by Jacques Cousteau among the top 10 diving sites in the world, the Poor Knights Islands lure underwater enthusiasts from all over the globe. The remnants of an ancient volcano, the islands are bathed in a warm ocean current from the north, making the surrounding waters a subtropical paradise for marine life. Schools of blue maomao swim among the colourful sponges, while stingrays patrol the numerous tunnels, grottoes and archways. Dive boats are regulars around the many coves and rocks, but there is no public access onto the islands themselves, which are protected above water as well as below.

NORTHLAND

New Zealand's petroleum products are refined at the Marsden Point Oil Refinery, near Whangarei. Giant tankers carry five million tonnes of crude oil to the wharf at the entrance to Whangarei Harbour each year. The refinery was constructed in 1964 in response to the country's growing passion for automobiles and the high price of imported petrol.

Whangarei (*overleaf*), 180 kilometres north of Auckland, is the urban centre of Northland. Situated at the head of a natural harbour and surrounded by farmland, its distinct flavour comes from its dual role as a busy agricultural service centre and a bustling port. From the inland suburb of Kamo, Whangarei Harbour seems landlocked, for the entrance at Marsden Point is only narrow, making the inlet a superb haven for trawlers and cruising yachts alike.

NEW ZEALAND FROM THE AIR

NORTHLAND

Auckland

The waters of Cape Rodney-Okakari Point, just north of Leigh, were the first in New Zealand to be designated a marine reserve. The reserve was created in 1977 as a sanctuary for sea life pressured by recreational fishers from Auckland, an hour's drive south. Within its borders, Goat Island offers refuge to blue penguins and other seabirds. Scientists at the University of Auckland Marine Laboratory carry out research into the area's rich underwater environment.

AUCKLAND

Tiny Beehive Island, south of its much larger neighbour, Kawau Island, is a breeding spot for the endangered New Zealand dotterel. It is also one of the few places in New Zealand free of kiore, the Pacific rat, which is a threat to many native bird species, including the dotterel. A member of the plover family, the dotterel makes its nest on the beach just above the high-tide line, making it easy prey for rats and other introduced predators, such as stoats. Beehive Island is also free of human beach-goers, whose presence can disturb ground-nesting birds.

Private boats, here at anchor in Bon Accord Harbour, are the principal means of transport to and from the mainland for residents of Kawau Island. Kawau was once the private property of Sir George Grey, a former governor of New Zealand. The English statesman purchased the island in 1862 and built a Georgian-style English country house in what became known as Mansion Bay. He transformed the island into a menagerie of exotic animals and plants. His living collection included Chinese pheasants, Californian quail, kookaburras, kangaroos, deer and even zebra.

Auckland spreads far to either side of Waitemata Harbour (*above*) and is now home to over a quarter of New Zealand's population. Eighty percent of New Zealanders are city-dwellers, with more than half living in the country's five major urban centres. The largest city in the South Pacific, Auckland has also become 'the capital of Polynesia', as Pacific Islanders have been drawn here by the prospect of employment. New Zealand is home to 82 percent of Niueans and 64 percent of Cook Islanders.

The youngest and most impressive of Auckland's 50 or so volcanoes is Rangitoto (*below*). Guarding the entrance to Waitemata Harbour, the island forms the backdrop to views from all over the city. It emerged from the sea about 600 years ago in a series of fiery explosions — an event witnessed by Maori on the mainland and the neighbouring island of Motutapu. As the lava cooled, it formed the black basaltic rock seen today. Despite the lack of soil, vegetation has spread across the island, which now supports the largest pohutukawa forest in New Zealand.

AUCKLAND

The Auckland Harbour Bridge opened in 1959, paving the way for the rapid expansion of the city's North Shore. Drivers crossing the bridge paid a toll until its abolition in 1984. The massive increase in traffic over the years resulted in the addition of extra lanes — dubbed 'the Nippon clip-ons' — on both sides of the bridge. The bridge is still the scene of daily tailbacks as rush-hour commuters pass from one side of the harbour to the other.

Takapuna is the business and commercial centre of Auckland's North Shore and East Coast Bays. Barely separated from the ocean, the freshwater Lake Pupuke is a flooded volcanic crater, while the intertidal lava reef nearby was formed during the same eruption. Like Auckland's many other volcanoes, Pupuke is extinct, and houses crowd round. Those fortunate enough to own a home overlooking the sea have some of Auckland's finest beaches on their doorstep.

Auckland's skyline has changed dramatically in recent years due to a spate of high-rise building development. The most obvious newcomer is the Sky Tower, part of the Sky City casino complex. Building began in 1994 and was completed in June 1997 amid considerable publicity. It stands 333.6 metres high and, at the time of opening, was the tallest building in the southern hemisphere. Floodlit at night, the tower provides an exciting focus for the central city.

Motuihe Island is only 16 kilometres by ferry from downtown Auckland and a popular spot for day-trippers. Earlier visitors were less impressed: during World War One the island's old quarantine complex was used as a prisoner-of-war camp. Probably its most famous internee was the German naval officer Count Felix von Luckner — the 'Sea Devil of the Southern Seas'. Captured in Fiji in 1917, von Luckner soon made good his escape, only to be recaptured eight days later off the Kermadec Islands.

AUCKLAND

Mt Eden, or Maungawhau, standing over downtown Auckland, is the highest point in the city and the most prominent of its mainland volcanoes. Being readily defended, it was once home to a fortified Maori settlement, or pa, of around 3000 people. Old gardening terraces and the indentations of storage pits for kumara — a sweet potato — remain visible round the summit. The hill is now a domain and a popular vantage-point for gazing out over the Auckland isthmus in all directions.

Brown's Island, or Motukorea, is one of the least modified of Auckland's volcanoes. Unlike nearby Rangitoto it has no native bush cover, so the structure of the crater is clearly visible. The island, once privately owned, has escaped numerous schemes for development, including an ill-advised plan to use it for refuse disposal. Archaeologists have identified three pa sites on the island.

AUCKLAND

Two small islands in Tamaki Strait, at the bottom of the Hauraki Gulf east of Auckland, are like stepping-stones to the larger Ponui and Waiheke Islands. Green Pakihi Island has avoided the fate of its tiny neighbour, Karamuramu Island, which has been stripped of its topsoil. A colony of North Island brown kiwi lives in the native bush on Ponui Island.

The marina at Halfmoon Bay harbours just a few of the countless recreational vessels on Auckland's waters. Known as 'The City of Sails', Auckland boasts more boats per capita than any other city in the world. Seamanship is a feature of both Maori and European culture, both peoples having discovered, explored and settled the country by sea. No part of New Zealand is more than two hours' drive from the coastline, and, for most New Zealanders, living far from the sea would be unthinkable.

NEW ZEALAND FROM THE AIR

AUCKLAND

Manukau Harbour is twice the size of Waitemata Harbour, but its shifting sandbars and narrow west-coast entrance make it difficult to navigate, and few vessels sail into it. Mangere Mountain (*inset*), Puketutu Island and nearby Mangere Lagoon — today the site of a series of sludge ponds — are three more of Auckland's volcanoes.

The maritime radio station at Musick Point, backed by the Howick Golf Course, enjoys a commanding view of the Hauraki Gulf. Built in 1938, it stands as a memorial to Captain Edwin Musick and his crew, whose Pan American flying-boat, the *Samoan Clipper*, exploded over the Pacific Ocean in 1939 while surveying the early San Francisco–Auckland air route. Pohutukawa trees cling to the surrounding cliffs. Known affectionately as the New Zealand Christmas tree, the pohutukawa blossoms bright crimson for a few short weeks in December.

Waikato

Green Island is the smallest of the Mercury Islands, off the eastern tip of the Coromandel Peninsula. Captain Cook named the islands after observing the transit of Mercury across the sun on the mainland nearby. Using data obtained on the opposite side of the planet, British scientists were able to calculate the planet's distance from the earth and the path of its orbit through space.

The Aldermen Islands, jutting out of the ocean to the east of the Coromandel Peninsula, are home to the tuatara, an ancient lizard that roamed the earth with the dinosaurs and has survived for millions of years in the isolation of New Zealand. Once common on the mainland, tuatara are now confined to a few offshore islands cared for by the Department of Conservation as wildlife sanctuaries. A permit is required to visit these islands.

WAIKATO

Cathedral Cove is tucked away on the east side of the Coromandel Peninsula, close to the small settlement of Hahei. Access is along a track that winds through groves of pohutukawa, puriri and other native trees and offers spectacular sea views. While holiday-makers flock in summer to the longer, sweeping bays further south — such as Pauanui, Whangamata and Waihi — the more rugged north of the peninsula saves its treasures for the more adventurous. The beaches of the Coromandel are also rich in gemstones such as jasper and agate.

The exposed peak of Castle Rock protrudes from the dense bush of the Coromandel Forest Park. The 72,000-hectare park spreads the length of the rugged mountain range that forms the backbone of the Coromandel Peninsula. To either side the coastline is a meandering arrangement of estuaries and bays, of secluded islands and secret coves. The rural lifestyle offered by the Coromandel attracts a variety of residents — artists and artisans, alternative-lifestylers and city folk in search of tranquillity — and the peninsula is a popular spot for holiday homes.

NEW ZEALAND FROM THE AIR

WAIKATO

The resort town of Pauanui (*previous page*) crowds over a shelf of land beside the Tairua River. Many of its houses are holiday homes, to which city residents come to unwind and enjoy the stunning ocean views. Walking trails wind their way over the bush-clad hills nearby, home to the kauri tree, coveted by the European settlers for its fine timber. Kauri can grow to be over a thousand years old, although few such giants remain today.

A sandbar at the edge of the surf links Hauturu Island to the beach at Whangamata, on the east coast of the Coromandel Peninsula. Whangamata, quiet for most of the year, is transformed in summer as surfers march onto the sand and big-game fishing launches head out into the Bay of Plenty. Common catches include kingfish, tuna, marlin and mako sharks. After the flurry of visitors has passed, the local inhabitants enjoy the mild winter with which the sun-drenched Coromandel coast is blessed.

Orchards flourish near Waihi, at the foot of the Coromandel Peninsula. Waihi became a wealthy gold-mining town following the discovery of gold on the Coromandel Peninsula in 1852. The precious metal was trapped in veins of quartz in solid rock, and could only be extracted after the quartz had been crushed in a stamper battery. Gold-mining became a large-scale enterprise, and when the last of Waihi's mines closed in 1952, gold (and some silver) to the current value of NZ$4 billion had been extracted. Open pit mining commenced in 1988 and continues today.

The rolling green fields of Matamata, in central Waikato, are popular with racehorse breeders and trainers, and home to many of New Zealand's internationally renowned steeds. Place names such as Cambridge, Lichfield and Shaftesbury speak of the English settlers' natural fondness for the Waikato's gentle landscape and mild climate. Yet such old-country gentility has far from extinguished the strong Maori character of the region, which was the scene of bitter conflict between British soldiers and Maori warriors over land ownership.

Hamilton, New Zealand's largest inland city, is bisected by the country's longest river, the Waikato, yet this natural waterway has never been developed as a serious transport route, either in the direction of Auckland to the north or to points south. The sites of most early settlements were chosen for their natural harbours, but Hamilton owes its existence to the fertile land in which it stands — land the European settlers had to confiscate from the region's powerful Maori tribes before turning it into pasture. As the area's agricultural potential was developed, so the city grew up over the deserted Maori village of Kirikirioa.

Waikato cows graze on some of the world's richest pasture. Dairy farming is the region's largest industry, producing some nine billion litres of milk a year, over 90 percent of which is exported as far afield as Europe and America, along with dairy products such as milk powder, cream and cheese. New Zealand leads the world in developing new milk products and dairy-farming techniques.

The small settlement of Raglan, 50 kilometres from Hamilton, serves as the land-locked city's seaside suburb. While the harbour offers fishing boats and launches a respite from the Tasman swell, surfers flock to Manu and Whale Bays to ride the rollers. The black-sand beaches of the Raglan coast were made famous in the 1960s surf movie *Endless Summer*.

Kawhia Harbour, south of Raglan, is where the ancestral Tainui canoe, carrying the founders of the many Waikato tribes, made landfall in New Zealand. The Polynesian settlers brought with them the kumara, a sweet potato that has since become a staple of New Zealand cuisine. Centuries later, the harbour was the rallying point for 5000 Maori warriors who came together to defeat Te Rauparaha, an enemy chief from the south. Despite its impressive natural harbour, the small town of Kawhia has escaped development and retains its flavour of times past.

NEW ZEALAND FROM THE AIR

WAIKATO

Taupo, nestled beside New Zealand's largest lake, enjoys a sweeping view across the water to the snow-capped volcanoes of Tongariro National Park. The waterfront (*inset*) is part of the Queen's Chain, a 20-metre-wide public reserve that borders New Zealand's entire coastline as well as its lakes and rivers. The lake itself fills the crater of a volcano many times larger than any other in the country. Taupo's most recent eruption — almost 2000 years ago, and one of the most violent of the last 5000 years anywhere in the world — threw a column of pumice, ash and rock 50 kilometres into the atmosphere. The volcano devastated the land for 90 kilometres in all directions — an area that today supports a population of 20,000. Places as distant as the bottom of the North Island, where Wellington now stands, were buried knee-deep in volcanic debris.

Soon after leaving Lake Taupo on its 354-kilometre journey to the Tasman Sea, the Waikato River is faced with a tight squeeze across an 11-metre shelf. The Huka Falls leap almost horizontally from the gap into the calmer water beyond. After these initial acrobatics, and the Aratiatia Rapids a short distance downstream, the Waikato continues in more sedate fashion.

The Kaingaroa Forest, sprawling north and south to the east of Taupo, is reputedly the world's largest man-made forest. Its 150,000 hectares of *Pinus radiata*, a native of California, supply logs to pulp and paper mills around the world. Forestry is New Zealand's third largest export earner, accounting for 13 percent of export sales, while New Zealand is set to overtake Chile as the world's largest producer of radiata pine.

The lakeside village of Kuratau lies 40 kilometres across the water from Taupo. Although the lake is a popular holiday spot, most of its shoreline remains undeveloped and accessible only by boat. Its aquamarine colour hints at its astonishing depth. In places the floor of the lake is almost 600 metres below the surface, nearly twice as deep as Cook Strait, which divides the North and South Islands.

NEW ZEALAND FROM THE AIR

WAIKATO

Mt Ruapehu and Mt Ngauruhoe loom over the Rangipo Desert on the North Island's volcanic plateau. Drivers on the Desert Road, part of State Highway 1, may catch a glimpse of New Zealand army personnel on manoeuvres in the bleak landscape. In winter, the road is often closed because of snow.

During the 1995 eruption of Mt Ruapehu, the crater lake was thrown out by a series of explosions, sending numerous lahars — streams of water and volcanic debris — pouring down the sides of the mountain. The crater continued to belch ash and, for a short time, glowing rocks, before settling to a steamy calm. At 2797 metres, Mt Ruapehu is the North Island's highest peak, although measured from its base on the central plateau it is not as tall as Mt Taranaki.

Mt Ruapehu's crater lake has emptied on more than one occasion. Most disastrously, part of the crater wall gave way on Christmas Eve 1953, allowing a flood of hot water, ash and boulders to sweep down the mountainside and demolish the railway bridge over the River Whangaehu at Tangiwai. A few minutes later the Auckland–Wellington express plunged into the river, killing 151 people.

WAIKATO

The perfectly shaped cone of Mt Ngauruhoe, 2287 metres high, comes second only to White Island as New Zealand's most active volcano, having erupted more than 60 times between 1839 and 1975. It has since been dormant, however, without even the plume of steam that commonly rose from its crater earlier in the century.

The eyes of the world turned to New Zealand in September 1995 as Mt Ruapehu suddenly burst into life (*right*) for only the second time in 50 years. The slopes were cleared of skiers and trampers as fears mounted that a major eruption might ensue. However, within a few weeks the volcano had settled down once more, and although ash had been carried as far as Hawke's Bay, only minor damage had been caused.

When Mt Ruapehu finished erupting, a lake began to collect in the crater once more. Ash blanketed the slopes (*right below*) where skiers and climbers had previously enjoyed snow and ice, but soon all was returned to pristine white, and little sign remained of the mountain's spectacular awakening. Yet the eruption was a reminder of the awesome natural forces that may be unleashed on the New Zealand landscape at any time.

Ash from the 1995 eruption of Mt Ruapehu was carried across the Tongariro River delta into Lake Taupo (*following*). Many of the waterways in the region, renowned for their trout fishing, were choked by ash. Their normally crystal-clear waters were turned an opaque grey, and many fish were lost as a result.

Bay of Plenty

Growing right down to the shoreline, the pine trees of Matakana Island are part of New Zealand's growing forestry industry. Across New Zealand, 1.6 million hectares of radiata pine earn $2.7 billion in annual exports. The introduced trees, which mature in less than 30 years, are planted in preference to slower-growing native species. In some areas, selective logging of native trees continues, although only a fraction of the country's original forest cover remains.

The green dome of Mt Maunganui stands guard over the entrance to Tauranga Harbour. Tauranga is the country's busiest port, hundreds of cargo ships heading in and out every year, to and from ports all around the world. The beach at Mt Maunganui becomes packed with surfers, swimmers and sunbathers in summer as New Zealanders flock to what is one of the country's most popular resorts.

At the edge of the ocean Mt Maunganui rises abruptly out of an otherwise almost uniformly flat landscape. The name Maunganui means 'large mountain', although, at only 230 metres high, this volcanic cone is little more than a modest hill. Nevertheless, it made an excellent defensive position for the local Maori in times past, affording a clear view of attackers in all directions. Today, a walking trail spirals round the hill, allowing easy access to the panoramic view from its summit.

Omokoroa Beach is a small settlement in Tauranga Harbour, just outside the port city. The name Tauranga means 'sheltered anchorage', something appreciated by the owners of many a big-game fishing launch. Tauranga's population of 90,000 enjoys a healthy economy, buoyed by the port facility and the region's orchards. The city's proximity to other major centres in the North Island, such as Rotorua and Hamilton, plus its pleasant climate, attract many New Zealanders to the area.

Motuhora Island, nine kilometres off the coast near Whakatane, in the Bay of Plenty, is an ancient volcano, although the only obvious signs of its explosive past are a few hot springs and fumaroles on its western side. It is also known as Whale Island because of its distinctive shape when seen from shore. Maori tribes lived here at the time of Captain Cook's circumnavigation of New Zealand, but the old settlement has long been abandoned and Motuhora Island is now the home of migrating birds.

In 1987, an enormous earthquake jolted the Bay of Plenty, ripping apart the farmland near Whakatane. Anything overlying the fault line was wrenched in two, from roads and railway tracks to paddocks and houses. The owners of this property (*right*), near Edgecumbe, were fortunate not to lose their farmhouse, built just metres from the fault line. An earthquake of magnitude six on the Richter scale occurs in New Zealand about once a year, while an earthquake of magnitude seven or more occurs about once every 10 years.

A column of steam rises from White Island (Whakaari), New Zealand's most active volcano. On a fine day the plume is visible from the mainland, 48 kilometres away at its nearest point, but relatively few people ever get a close-up view of the island. Twelve lives were lost in 1914 during an attempt to mine sulphur on the island — only the camp cat survived. Despite its offshore location, White Island lies on the Taupo Volcanic Zone, which extends across the centre of the North Island. Its true size is masked by the ocean, which covers 70 percent of its bulk.

The crater of White Island is a volatile arena of billowing fumaroles and boiling mud pools. Continuously transforming itself, it is a dangerous place for visitors. Geysers can suddenly gush from the ground, showering the surrounding area with droplets of stinging acid. Visits should only be undertaken with an experienced guide. Both charter-boat and helicopter trips are available.

NEW ZEALAND FROM THE AIR

Rotorua (*opposite above*) is New Zealand's prime tourism hot spot. With its hot springs, steaming geysers and bubbling mud pools, it is on every visitor's itinerary — especially the majestic Pohutu geyser, which plays to a height of 30 metres or more in the Whakarewarewa thermal park. Rotorua also showcases Maori culture, the centrepiece of which is the Maori Arts and Crafts Institute and model village at Whakarewarewa. Lake Rotorua itself is a drowned volcanic crater.

A veil of steam hangs over the Champagne Pool (*opposite below*), a hot spring in the Waiotapu thermal area. The pool is named after the way it fizzes with tiny gas bubbles that rise from its depths. Waiotapu, or 'Sacred Waters', is south of Rotorua on the road to Taupo.

Three thermal lakes (*right*) near Waimangu, south of Rotorua, line up before Mt Tarawera and Lake Rotomahana. In the foreground is the Southern Crater, with the steaming Frying Pan Lake and the smaller Inferno Crater beyond. With a surface area of 38,000 square metres, Frying Pan Lake is the world's largest hot spring. At its deepest point the water reaches a temperature of 200°C.

Mt Tarawera, thought to be an extinct volcano, suddenly burst into life in the early hours of 10 June 1886. The eruption destroyed three Maori villages and killed 153 people. The previously flat mountain summit was rent apart, forming a series of craters about 5 kilometres long, while further vents were blown out in a southwesterly direction for another 12 kilometres or so. The eruption also destroyed the famous Pink and White Terraces, two enormous sinter deposits, created by hot springs, that adorned the mountain slopes above Lake Rotomahana like a pair of sweeping staircases. The terraces were an early tourist attraction — perhaps New Zealand's greatest ever. Today, visitors can take scenic flights and 4WD tours to the area.

A tourist boat visits a steaming cliff on Lake Rotomahana, near the now submerged site of the Pink and White Terraces. Eleven days before the eruption of Mt Tarawera in 1886, passengers aboard two tourist boats on their way to the terraces reported seeing a Maori canoe, or waka, paddle past. As no such canoe existed on the lake, local Maori regarded the sighting as an apparition and an omen of disaster.

A boardwalk over the Warbrick Terraces, in the Waimangu thermal area, allows visitors to explore the volcanic springs without damaging the site. The terraces are a colourful combination of hydroxide silicate and iron oxide overgrown by algae. The terraces are named after Alf Warbrick, one of the founders of tourism in Rotorua.

The silica terraces of Lake Ohakuri are a lesser version of the Pink and White Terraces destroyed in the 1886 eruption of Mt Tarawera. A small tourist boat shuttles visitors to and from the site but, due to its remote location, it remains one of the least visited spots in the Rotorua area. Lake Ohakuri is a flooded section of the Waikato River, north of Taupo, created by one of a series of hydro-electricity dams. The lower portion of the terraces is submerged, but the more spectacular upper part remains above water.

The bubbling springs at Orakei Korako, between Rotorua and Taupo, cloud the air above with steam. Other gaseous emissions are invisible yet far from unnoticeable. The pungent smell of hydrogen sulphide — not unlike the stench of rotten eggs — permeates the air in most thermal areas, particularly in and around Rotorua. But while it may be bothersome on arrival, visitors soon become inured to its lingering presence.

Gisborne

Te Urewera National Park is the largest stretch of untouched native forest in the North Island, with a rich heritage of Maori history and legend. Most of the country's forest cover was cleared to make pasture for grazing, and today only a fraction of the bush that once clothed the land remains. Like all New Zealand's national parks, Te Urewera has a network of walking trails, including the 51-kilometre track round Lake Waikaremoana, that offer the visitor an unforgettable wilderness experience.

The East Cape is one of the most rugged and remote parts of the North Island. Much of the interior is covered with brooding, primeval forest; elsewhere land cleared for farming suffers severe erosion. Maori tradition tells how several of the ancestral canoes first came to shore here, and the descendants of those early settlers remain a powerful presence across the region. The East Cape lighthouse stands atop the cliffs at the mainland's most easterly point.

At 1752 metres above sea level, the summit of Mt Hikurangi is the highest point on the East Cape and the highest non-volcanic mountain in the North Island. The name Hikurangi means 'summit of the sky', and was conferred in memory of a mountain on Hawai'iki, the legendary island home of the Maori explorers. With a view far across the ocean to the east, Mt Hikurangi is the first spot in New Zealand to catch the light of dawn.

GISBORNE

Young Nick's Head is where Captain Cook's first voyage round New Zealand began. As his ship, *Endeavour*, approached from Tahiti, all eyes on board strained to see land, and it was Nicholas Young, the surgeon's boy, whose cry went up first. The explorers ventured ashore in the sweeping bay immediately north of the head, encountering the local Maori, who had observed *Endeavour*'s arrival. Relations between the two peoples got off to a bad start. Disputes broke out, leading to bloodshed when Cook's men killed six warriors. As he sailed away, filled with disappointment at the turn of events, Cook named the place at which he had landed Poverty Bay, 'because it afforded us no one thing we wanted'.

The area round Gisborne, New Zealand's most easterly city, remains justly proud of its Maori heritage. Nearly half its population is Maori — the highest proportion of any city in the country. While not such a tourist-oriented focus of Maori culture as the more central Rotorua region, Gisborne is one of the few places in the country where the language of its Polynesian settlers is still commonly spoken.

Sediment deposited by the sluggish Waipaoa River as it meanders its way to the ocean at Poverty Bay has created the nutrient-rich Waipaoa Flats. Here the excellent soil and warm, humid climate nurture many orchards and vineyards. Citrus fruits, kiwifruit, chardonnay, gewürztraminer — these are just some of the region's mouth-watering delights. Gisborne's distinctive wines enjoy an international reputation and are deservedly popular throughout New Zealand.

Hawke's Bay

Summer in Napier brings days of endless sunshine. In the balmy sea air, visitors can stroll along Marine Parade, the tree-lined waterfront boulevard, enjoying an array of shops, markets, street acts and other entertainments. But Napier is best known for its architecture. Following the city's destruction by an earthquake in 1931, it was entirely rebuilt, much of it in the Art Deco style popular at the time. An annual festival celebrates this special heritage, while guided walks visit some of the finer buildings.

In its early days, Napier was a small town hard up against the southern side of Bluff Hill and almost surrounded by a tidal lagoon, from which land for expansion had to be reclaimed. An unexpected benefit of the devastating earthquake of 1931, which reduced the town to rubble and killed 256 people, was the partial draining of the lagoon as an area of some 3400 hectares was raised by one to three metres. New dry land was instantly available, allowing the development of, among other things, a dockyard and the suburb of Westshore.

A short distance south of Napier, the Tutaekuri and Ngaruroro Rivers merge in a lagoon separated from the ocean by a sandbar. The rivers flow between Napier and its close neighbour, Hastings. Despite their proximity, the cities have distinctive personalities: Hastings, surrounded by orchards and food-processing factories, is the region's agricultural hub, while Napier is the port. Expansion from both directions threatens to spread across the rivers and join the two centres in an uninterrupted urban sprawl.

The long, southward sweep of Hawke Bay ends at Cape Kidnappers. From October to April, the clifftops are home to one of the world's few mainland gannet colonies. Usually these seabirds — which plunge into the water for fish at speeds of up to 130 kilometres an hour — congregate on offshore stacks and islands, where there is less risk of attack from predators. Captain Cook gave the cape its unusual name after an incident in which local Maori tried to make off with a Polynesian servant boy from *Endeavour*.

A cluster of houses faces the pounding surf of Ocean Beach, south of Hastings. For generations New Zealanders have built holiday homes — called baches in the North Island and cribs in the South — close to the sea where peace and solitude reign. With a carload of gear and supplies — fishing rods a must — they flee the city to enjoy the outdoors and the simple comforts of four walls and a tin chimney. Increasingly people are choosing to holiday overseas, yet nothing compares with the timeless pleasure of a weekend 'at the bach'.

Lake Poukawa, some 20 kilometres inland from Ocean Beach, lies in an unusually wide valley for the eastern side of the North Island. From Hawke's Bay down to Cape Palliser, the land has been crumpled into an endless succession of rugged hill ranges, now largely stripped of bush and sown with pasture. One hill, about 50 kilometres south of Lake Poukawa, proudly bears what is purported to be the longest place name in the world: Taumatawhaka-tangihangakoauauotamateaturipukakapikimaungahoronukupokaiwhenua-kitanatahu. Translated, the 85-letter name means: 'The place where Tamatea, the man with big knees who slid, climbed and swallowed mountains, known as land-eater, played his flute to his loved one'.

Taranaki

The Three Sisters stand sentinel near the mouth of the Tongaporutu River, facing the North Taranaki Bight. In some of the nearby caverns, hollowed out from the cliffs by the sea, are examples of early Maori rock art.

NEW ZEALAND FROM THE AIR

The white cliffs near the small coastal settlement of Pukearuhe, north of New Plymouth, rise sheer from a black ironsand beach. Trampers can enjoy the sea air along the 10-kilometre White Cliffs Walkway between the Tongaporutu River and Pukearuhe. This photograph was taken from a helicopter hovering just above the waves.

NEW ZEALAND FROM THE AIR

TARANAKI

Taranaki (also known as Mt Egmont) (*above*), a classic cone-shaped volcano, rises from a circular plain on the North Island's west coast. At 2518 metres high, it is the North Island's tallest volcano. It last erupted in 1642, just before the arrival of the Dutch explorer Abel Tasman, yet Tasman, who sailed along the Taranaki coast on his way north, failed to notice the mountain, which was shrouded in cloud. Weather conditions on Taranaki are notoriously changeable, and a hazard to those who venture towards the summit. Many climbers have lost their lives on the treacherous slopes.

The two spherical formations on the southern slopes of Taranaki, known as the Beehives (*opposite*), were formed when lava oozed from the volcano's flank. They are estimated to be 1300 years old. As arresting as any of the mountain's geological features is the distinctive flora that clothes its slopes, from lush sub-alpine forest around its base — the province of towering rimu and rata trees — to alpine herbfields above the bush line. Egmont National Park, with more than 140 kilometres of walking tracks, is centred round the dormant volcano.

NEW ZEALAND FROM THE AIR

TARANAKI

The fertile Taranaki plain ends abruptly at the coastal cliffs near Manaia. Once carpeted with forest, the plain now rivals the Waikato region as the best grazing in the land and supports some of New Zealand's most productive herds. The discovery of vast fields of natural gas both on- and offshore has lifted the region's economy, but its prolific dairy industry remains its primary earner.

Manawatu and Wanganui

State Highway 1 weaves its way through steep hill country near Mangaweka, between the central plateau and the Manawatu plains. The country's main arterial road runs from Cape Reinga in the Far North to Bluff at the foot of the South Island. New Zealand's mountainous terrain makes road construction difficult, and drivers have to contend with tight corners and narrow stretches, even on the premier highway.

Dividing the Wanganui and Taranaki regions, the Patea River travels a long, meandering course to the coastal town of Patea. Few settlements interrupt the dense forest that cloaks its banks.

Wanganui, at the mouth of the Whanganui River used to be a major port and a gateway to the interior of the North Island. Steamers carried people and goods up and down the river, the country's longest navigable waterway, until the late 1950s, but today serve as a tourist attraction, along with jet boats, canoes and kayaks.

Wellington

The Manawatu plains extend down the coast towards Wellington. At Otaki the river of the same name slices through the green fields to the sea. Today a busy market-gardening centre, Otaki was once the mainland base of the warrior Te Rauparaha. The many marae — areas of tribal land each with a whare, or meeting house, on it — near the town testify to the continuing strong presence of Maori in the region.

Part of a chain of seaside settlements along the Kapiti Coast, famous for its cheeses, fruit and vegetables, Waikanae Beach is a popular retirement spot. Nearby Kapiti Island was once the stronghold of Ngati Toa chief Te Rauparaha, dubbed the Maori Napoleon. Born in 1768, Te Rauparaha led his warriors on a warpath round much of the country, destroying villages and slaughtering rival tribes. Of neither high social rank nor imposing physique, he was nevertheless a brilliant strategist and intent on conquest. Maori as far afield as the bottom of the South Island suffered at his hands, and he was a constant provocation to European settlers in the Wellington region.

Five kilometres from the coast, Kapiti Island today is a bird sanctuary, providing a safe environment for many of New Zealand's native species, including kiwi. The island has been cleared of introduced pests, including rats, which prey on eggs and chicks, and possums, which kill the trees they graze on. Since its introduction from Australia last century, the ring-tailed possum has spread through New Zealand's forests until there are now more than 70 million animals.

Clouds mass against the Tararua Range, a dazzling expanse of cotton-wool softness from above but bringing rain to those below. The Tararuas, together with the Ruahines to the north and the Rimutakas to the south, form the backbone of the lower North Island. Their rugged, forested interior has much to offer the keen tramper, but the steep slopes and frequently severe weather can make conditions treacherous.

Greytown, named after Governor George Grey, was the first major settlement on the Wairarapa plain and a provincial capital for the region's farming community. The country's earliest pastoral farming took place to the south, on the eastern shores of Lake Wairarapa, an area that lent itself readily to sheep-grazing. Further north the forested terrain proved more unyielding, and today's manicured pastures and orchards are the legacy of much physical labour and heartbreak.

WELLINGTON

The lighthouse at Castlepoint is a signal to ships approaching from the north and east that they are nearing Cook Strait, between the North and South Islands. Built in 1913, it stands 23 metres above its rock base and over 50 metres above the sea. The small seaside settlement is one of very few along what is for the most part a bleak and wild coastline. Locals gather on the sand in festive atmosphere for a picnic and a punt at Castlepoint's annual beach races.

The winds that gust through the Wairarapa hill country power the turbines of New Zealand's first wind farm, southeast of Martinborough. The seven generators, erected in 1996, provide enough electricity for 1500 homes — six percent of the region's power needs. Encouraged by the success of the operation, power companies are constructing larger farms, offering consumers a new and environmentally friendly source of energy.

The sweep of Palliser Bay's Ocean Beach marks the southern limit of the Wairarapa plain. The meandering Ruamahanga River empties into Lake Onoke before finally spilling through the surf into the Pacific Ocean. Along the horizon loom the remote Aorangi Mountains, where visitors to the Haurangi Forest Park can enjoy some rough terrain and a spectacular coastline.

NEW ZEALAND FROM THE AIR

Clearly visible in an aerial view of Wellington, New Zealand's capital (*above*), is the fault that runs down the edge of the Hutt Valley and through the city centre. Minor earthquakes are a frequent occurrence in Wellington and no cause for alarm. The last major quake was in 1855, a jolt which lifted much of the land in the area by several metres. Miramar Peninsula, next to the harbour entrance, was an island until the earthquake raised the adjacent seafloor, creating the neck of land on which Wellington airport has since been built.

The Hutt Valley (*opposite above*) was a swamp when Wellington's first city planners arrived in 1840. Fifteen years later, the powerful earthquake that rocked the young settlement they had built round Lambton Harbour lifted the valley floor by more than a metre. The swamp waters drained away, leaving an expansive area of flat land. While developers in the original town, crowded in by hills, worked to reclaim land from the sea, the Hutt Valley saw the spread of the spacious satellite centres of Lower and Upper Hutt.

Greater Wellington extends not only up the Hutt Valley but also through the Ngauranga Gorge to Porirua Harbour and the suburbs of Titahi Bay, Paremata, Plimmerton and Porirua (*opposite below*). The nearly continuous urban sprawl sees many commuters make the daily journey over the hills to the central city.

WELLINGTON

WELLINGTON

Lambton Harbour (*previous*) is the heart of Wellington, its waterfront being home to some of the city's leading attractions. Opened in 1998, the national museum, Te Papa, showcases Maori, European and natural history, and mounts a wide range of art exhibitions. Further along the waterfront are Frank Kitts Park and the Queen's Wharf Event Centre. A little further back is Civic Square, where the town hall, library and art gallery face each other.

The Wellington suburb of Roseneath looks down on Evan's Bay to one side and Oriental Bay on the other. Wellingtonians are at home in the hills, often living in houses built on stilts and parking their cars on steep inclines. Even in the city's few flat areas they sometimes have to walk leaning into the gale-force winds for which Wellington is notorious.

WELLINGTON

Downtown Wellington, much of it on reclaimed land, is hemmed in by the Tinakori slopes behind and the harbour in front. Construction is subject to special regulations because of the risk of earthquakes. The maze of narrow streets and stairways can be disorienting for outsiders, but the resident population of 350,000 enjoys the tight jumble of what is the nation's artistic and cultural centre as well as its administrative focus.

Wellington's Oriental Parade curves out from the edge of the city centre. Halfway round, diners in the pavilion restaurant over the beach enjoy a panoramic view past the Carter Memorial Fountain and across the harbour. The parade is popular with joggers, walkers and roller-bladers, particularly during the weekday lunch hour, when city workers take the opportunity to exercise while enjoying as sweeping a vista as any city can offer.

The battered coastline at Owhiro Bay, overlooking Cook Strait, is only minutes from downtown Wellington. Known as Red Rocks for the cluster of rocks coloured with red algae, the bay is a popular walking spot, with a track running beneath the cliffs as far as Sinclair Head. It is also home to a seal colony, and the animals can be seen lounging on the shore near the high-tide mark.

Nelson and Tasman

Farewell Spit stretches eastwards from the South Island's most northerly point 30 kilometres into the fierce currents of Cook Strait. Sediments transported up the West Coast have steadily accumulated to form its slender curve. To the south of its protective reach, home to the migrating Siberian godwit, are the waters of Golden Bay. Before the construction of a lighthouse at the spit's distant end, the sandbar was a menace to seafarers, causing many a ship to run aground.

At the mouth of the Aorere River, Collingwood marks the final frontier at the top of the South Island: beyond lie only wilderness and the very smallest of settlements. The town was founded in the gold-rush days and served briefly as the main port for diggers arriving from Australia. When the rush ended, Collingwood sank into obscurity, a lonely outpost at the end of the road. But today, as the gateway south to Kahurangi National Park and the gateway north to Farewell Spit, Collingwood has become a headquarters for tramping and nature safaris.

Wainui Bay, on the western tip of Abel Tasman National Park, is where Tasman anchored his two ships, *Heemskerk* and *Zeehaan*, in 1642, setting the scene for the first encounter between European and Maori. It was a bloody occasion. Four sailors were killed in a brief skirmish when their cockle-boat, passing between the two vessels, was attacked by a party of warriors in a canoe. In the face of such hostility, Tasman left New Zealand without attempting to land.

Along the scalloped coast of the Abel Tasman National Park, bush meets sea in some of the country's most tranquil and inviting beaches. The park, created in 1942, bears the name of the Dutch explorer who, 300 years earlier, was the first European to arrive in New Zealand waters, although the French navigator Dumont d'Urville was the first European to properly explore the area. Today the park is popular for its easy walking track and golden sands.

The Anchorage, in Torrent Bay, is as serene a spot as any in Abel Tasman National Park. The park is best explored on foot or by kayak. A 51-kilometre walking track winds round the coast, with huts and camp sites along the way for overnight breaks. For kayakers, the sea is usually calm and allows for a leisurely paddle.

Bark Bay is flanked by the smaller inlets of Mosquito Bay and Sandfly Bay — named after two of Abel Tasman National Park's more irksome inhabitants. Few visitors depart without having been paid a visit by one or other of the little critters.

Marahau is the main point of access to Abel Tasman National Park. Boat shuttles leave the town for points along the coastal track, carrying day walkers into the park in the morning and returning to collect them in the evening. Marahau is also the departure point for kayakers. The park is now so popular at the height of the summer season that visitors may soon be required to book their walk in advance.

The orchards of Moutere, south of Motueka, grow some of the country's highest-quality apples, pears and kiwifruit. Although much of the finest produce is reserved for lucrative international markets, such as Japan and Europe, visitors travelling through the countryside can buy plenty of fresh fruit at the many roadside stalls.

Red Hills Ridge (*above*) rises high above the tree line in Mt Richmond Forest Park, behind Nelson, but to the west grow the pine forests that stand at the heart of the Nelson economy. Forestry is one of New Zealand's most important industries — a dependable source of revenue at a time when sheep and dairy farming are in decline.

The end of the 13-kilometre-long Boulder Bank marks the entrance to Nelson Haven. In 1858, with a population of 2500, Nelson was New Zealand's largest settlement after Christchurch, but it grew only slowly and soon lagged well behind Canterbury's 'garden city' and Dunedin to the south. It has since blossomed into an arts and crafts centre, its artists and artisans producing everything from pottery and glassware to furniture and jewellery. Nelson is also where the country's first game of rugby football was played.

NELSON AND TASMAN

From Cable Bay, where the telegraph cable laid between Australia and New Zealand in 1876 came ashore, mud flats extend round Pepin Island to neighbouring Delaware Bay. The bay, which housed the telegraphic service until 1917, was also on the receiving end of Te Rauparaha and his warriors who crossed Cook Strait in 1828 and invaded the local Ngati Apa tribe. Ngati Apa paid dearly for their resistance at Cable Bay and were virtually wiped out by the overwhelming strength of the Ngati Toa warriors.

Marlborough

The Marlborough Sounds, at the top of the South Island, are a cruising paradise for yachts and launches. In the labyrinth of islands and inlets are many secluded coves and undisturbed beaches. Residents of the sounds are a self-reliant breed, as there are few roads and most people have to generate their own electricity and collect their own water. The sounds were formed after the last ice age as the sea level rose, drowning a series of dry valleys and leaving the mountain ridges in between above water.

The crooked finger of Long Island, at the head of Queen Charlotte Sound, points to the open sea. Beyond, Cape Koamaru marks the sound's eastern limit. Captain Cook visited Queen Charlotte Sound five times, and many place names, such as Ship Cove, Resolution Bay and Endeavour Inlet, record his passing. Other explorers have also left their mark, notably the Frenchman Dumont d'Urville, who in 1827 charted much of the intricate coastline and named Cape Soucis, Croisilles Harbour, French Pass and D'Urville Island.

The Cook Strait ferries cross paths where the Tory Channel enters Queen Charlotte Sound. Shuttling passengers, cars and trains back and forth between Picton and Wellington, the ferries travel almost non-stop, day and night. Although the strait is a mere 23 kilometres across at its narrowest point, exiting Wellington harbour and weaving through the sounds add considerably to the distance, and the journey takes a leisurely three hours. Modern catamarans make the crossing in half this time.

MARLBOROUGH

Picton (*opposite above*) became the gateway to the South Island in 1962, when regular ferry services across Cook Strait began. The ferry terminal welcomes hundreds of passengers a day to the country's larger half, fondly referred to as the Mainland by those who live there. The South Island accounts for 56 percent of the country's land area but only 30 percent of its population.

The hills and valleys that extend southwards from the Marlborough Sounds end abruptly at the Wairau Plains and the gentle curve of Cloudy Bay (*opposite below*). Here, rich alluvial soils beside the Wairau River provide fertile ground for some of the country's finest wine-makers. Many a Marlborough sauvignon blanc, in particular, has enjoyed deserved international acclaim. The region's wineries range from some of the country's largest to small, family-run affairs.

The evaporation ponds round Lake Grassmere (*above*), at the southern end of Clifford Bay, provide enough salt for New Zealand's total salt requirements. High temperatures and steady winds combine to produce optimal conditions for evaporation, and as much as 6000 tonnes of salt may be harvested a day, most of it for industrial purposes. Microalgae and tiny shrimps inhabit the ponds, and in the highly saline conditions may turn red, colouring the water.

Canterbury

River sediment, carried from as far inland as the Spencer Mountains, flows from the Clarence River into the sea north of Kaikoura, where the inshore currents prevent it from dispersing evenly.

The sea around Kaikoura Peninsula (*opposite*), which plummets to a depth of 1000 metres, is a Mecca for marine-mammal enthusiasts. Whale-watching tours take visitors to see sperm whales, dolphins and orca (killer whales), while the peninsula is also home to a large colony of New Zealand fur seals. The name Kaikoura means 'to eat crayfish', and this lobster-like delicacy, when in season, can be bought at the roadside ready cooked.

CANTERBURY

NEW ZEALAND FROM THE AIR

The Seaward Kaikoura Range, overlooking the east coast, is the outermost segment at the top end of the Southern Alps, which extend virtually the length of the South Island. Reaching almost 2600 metres in height, it lies parallel to the Inland Kaikoura Range, with the Clarence River flowing down the valley in between.

The mouth of the Waimakariri River, north of Christchurch, was once the city's main harbour, since superseded by Lyttelton. The area was also home to over 1000 Ngai Tahu, whose settlement on the river, Kaiapohia, was devastated by the North Island invader Te Rauparaha.

Like the spokes of a wheel, nine country roads meet at Charing Cross in the heart of the Canterbury Plain. Although the rich alluvial soil here is ideal for crop farming, this form of agriculture is not big business in New Zealand, most of the country being too mountainous. Nearly all crops grown locally are destined for the domestic market.

CANTERBURY

Christchurch is the South Island's largest city, with a population of 310,000. Its elegance is the legacy of English pioneers who set out to create 'the most English city outside England'. Four ships of settlers, supported by the Church of England, arrived in 1850 intent on securing an Anglican stronghold in the southern hemisphere. Today Christchurch is known as the 'Garden City' for its many public parks and well-trimmed private gardens.

NEW ZEALAND FROM THE AIR

The Avon River meanders through the Christchurch suburb of Dallington. A total of 37 bridges span the Avon in the space of 24 kilometres as it flows from one side of the city to the other. The willow trees along the banks have been grown from cuttings brought from St Helena, the island on which exiled French emperor Napoleon Bonaparte passed his last days.

Christchurch's Avon and Heathcote rivers share a large estuary at the edge of the city, which drains into the sea round the Spit at the end of the Sumner Bar. The suburb of Southshore, nearest the Spit, merges with New Brighton at the far end of the bar. The seaward shore marks the lower reaches of Pegasus Bay.

The Christchurch suburb of Scarborough Hill, perched above the cliffs of Sumner Head, affords exceptional views for a mostly flat city. It occupies the eastern extremity of the Port Hills, which rise suddenly along the southern edge of the city where the Canterbury Plain meets Banks Peninsula.

NEW ZEALAND FROM THE AIR

B anks Peninsula, the remains of two volcanic mountains, was once an island. It has become joined to the mainland by the advance of the Canterbury Plain, an accumulation of material eroded from the distant Southern Alps. Today the peninsula's flooded craters make fine natural harbours. Akaroa Harbour, in the foreground, attracted French settlers before being annexed by the British in 1840. Lyttelton Harbour serves as a port for neighbouring Christchurch.

P ompey's Pillar (*following*) juts from the cliffs on the southeast side of Bank's Peninsula. Much of the peninsula's craggy coast is inaccessible by road, but rewarding to those who make the effort to clamber down to any of the small hidden beaches. Captain Cook named the peninsula in honour of naturalist Joseph Banks, who accompanied him on *Endeavour* and helped finance the voyage.

Before Lyttelton Harbour could be of much use to Christchurch, the natural barrier of the Port Hills (*above*) had to be surmounted. The city's pioneers overcame the problem in 1867 by building a two-kilometre railway tunnel through the hills. At once Lyttelton became a busy port, serving not only the Canterbury Plains but also the West Coast, which was without a harbour. A road tunnel, parallel to the railway and the longest in the country, was opened in 1964.

The Rangitata River (*opposite above*), its headwaters in the Southern Alps just north of Mt Cook National Park, spills through the high-country sheep station known as Erewhon — the name being an anagram of 'nowhere'. The English novelist Samuel Butler came to New Zealand in 1860 and set off for the mountains on foot to establish the station. During his solitary life there, he built himself a cottage and weathered the cold storms and bitter winds on his own. After four years he sold the station at a huge profit and returned to England, where his experiences formed the inspiration of his novel *Erewhon*.

The Rakaia River (*opposite below*) is one of several great rivers that run in braided channels from the snow-capped Southern Alps across the fertile Canterbury Plain to the ocean.

The Duncan Stream (*left*), in the Ben Ohau Range on the eastern side of the Southern Alps, waits for rain. Unlike the wet West Coast, the eastern alps have a dry climate and are characteristically brown and barren. The area is known as the Mackenzie Country, after a Scottish settler accused of stealing sheep to stock his own run. Legend tells how the man's dog, Friday, his tongue removed to keep him from barking, was taken to the court, where he ran to his master's side, thereby giving him away.

With its man-made harbour, Timaru (*below*) is the heart of the South Canterbury economy. Yet it was not always so. Shingle carried up the coast from the Waitaki River and deposited inshore near the town made the siting and building of a harbour difficult. Debate on the matter continued until 1936, when the shingle was eventually used to reclaim 41 hectares of land as part of the construction, after which Timaru quickly became one of the country's busiest ports.

West Coast

At the top of the West Coast, the Heaphy River ends its journey to the Tasman Sea. Breaking from the bush of Kahurangi National Park alongside the river before heading south down the coast is the Heaphy Track, one of New Zealand's most popular walking routes. The track runs from near Collingwood, in Golden Bay, and makes its way through magnificent stands of native bush and across the red tussock of the Gouland Downs before the coastal stretch where palms and ferns lend a tropical flavour. The track takes four to six days to complete.

NEW ZEALAND FROM THE AIR

The Pororari River flows from the dense bush of the Paparoa National Park at Punakaiki. Early settlers were thwarted in their efforts to farm the region by the rugged terrain and harsh climate, and, discouraged, most left for more benevolent parts. The forest has since reclaimed much of the land it lost to axe and saw.

On a coastline short of natural harbours and renowned for foul weather, the Buller River at Westport provides welcome shelter for ships. The town's role as a port serving the whole West Coast has seen it survive the region's economic ups and downs. First came the rush for gold in the 1860s. After the precious metal had run out, the discovery of coal fuelled a new industry. Output peaked in 1920, then slowly decreased as production became uneconomical and demand waned. Huge coal deposits remain but are unlikely ever to be exploited. The unspoiled beauty of the West Coast, and the tourism it attracts, may hold the best prospects for future prosperity.

The Pancake Rocks, just outside Punakaiki, are a popular attraction for visitors to the West Coast. Horizontal sheets of limestone have been sculpted by sea and rain into curious pillars, like piles of pancakes. These are penetrated by passages, hollows and blowholes, which funnel the waves and compress the air trapped in them. At their most spectacular they throw up geyser-like spouts of water to the accompaniment of whiplash cracks, heavy thumps and reverberating booms.

The Crooked River delta on Lake Brunner, inland from the West Coast town of Greymouth, is a popular spot with anglers. The plentiful trout they seek are, like themselves, relative newcomers, having been introduced in the latter part of the nineteenth century. But another resident of the lake was here long before either — the rare and almost mystical white heron. Hence the Maori name for these peaceful waters — Moana Kotuku, 'Lake of the White Heron'.

WEST COAST

One of the few routes over the Southern Alps, the Arthur's Pass road (*opposite*) reaches an altitude of 920 metres. The original zigzag road, shown here with its steep hairpin bends, followed the trail blazed by Arthur Dudley Dobson when he discovered the pass while still only a teenager. Modern engineering has since simplified the journey.

Hokitika (*right*) is the greenstone centre of New Zealand. Long before Europeans arrived, Maori from all over Aotearoa made the arduous journey to this isolated part of the West Coast in search of the lustrous stone they called pounamu. From it they crafted weapons, ornaments and tools. Today it is retrieved from the streams and mountains by helicopter, and a thriving industry in the manufacture of greenstone items caters to the tourist trade. Greenstone is a rare form of nephrite, and so hard it has to be cut with diamond saws.

In heavy rain, the West Coast gushes water as creeks swell and riverbanks overflow. As the rain subsides, the waters slow and streams meander lazily through the wetlands. Certain plants thrive in this watery environment, such as kahikatea, or white pine, and the ubiquitous flax, or harakeke.

WEST COAST

The Franz Josef Glacier descends from the snowfield at its head, 2700 metres above sea level, into the valley it carved out for itself in ice ages past. Its snout is just 300 metres above sea level, making it readily accessible and a popular destination for tourists travelling up and down the West Coast. The glacier was named after the emperor of Austria by explorer Julius von Haast. A glacier is a slowly moving mass of ice, formed from compacted snow and driven by the force of gravity. As it moves, the ice buckles and cracks, opening up crevasses — an obvious hazard to anyone who ventures onto its surface.

The 15-kilometre-long Fox Glacier reaches from the heights of the Southern Alps down to the forested West Coast a short distance south of Franz Josef Glacier, and is equally accessible from the main road. Altogether there are some 350 glaciers in the alps, most within a 150-kilometre radius of Mt Cook. Over the millennia, they have sculpted the deep U-shaped valleys that characterise the massed ranges extending the length of the South Island.

State Highway 6, the main road up the West Coast, clings to the coastline as it weaves its way round Knight's Point, from where it heads inland. In the frequent heavy rain that drenches the West Coast the road is often closed by slips. It was first blocked by a landslide just hours after its official opening in 1965. Constant maintenance is required to keep the Coast's only road link to the outside world open.

Although marginally lower than their European namesakes, the Southern Alps are steeper. From beside the thin shelf of the West Coast, their jagged peaks rise abruptly into the sky. As Abel Tasman sailed past in 1642 he saw what he considered an inhospitable country, walled in by the spectacular mountain range. The Tasman Glacier, with its beginnings in snowfields close to the border of the Mt Cook and Westland National Parks, is the longest glacier in the temperate world, extending almost 30 kilometres down its valley.

NEW ZEALAND FROM THE AIR

WEST COAST

Standing 3754 metres above sea level, Mt Cook is the highest peak in Australasia. Its Maori name is Aoraki, meaning 'cloud piercer'. The mountain is the central attraction of Mt Cook National Park, within the boundaries of which are all but five of the country's peaks over 3050 metres high. The summit of Mt Cook was first scaled on Christmas Day 1894, and has been a mountaineer's Mecca ever since.

Under the looming flanks of the Southern Alps, and almost smothered by forest, the tiny West Coast township of Haast is reduced to insignificance. With a population of barely 200, Haast is a true frontier town, set on the edge of a vast wilderness — one of the world's great natural wonders and one of two World Heritage Sites in New Zealand. A visitors' centre provides information on the area, known as Te Waipounamu, meaning 'the place of the greenstone' and the Maori name for the South Island. The heritage site is a combination of four national parks — Mt Cook, Fiordland, Mt Aspiring and Westland. UNESCO is responsible for selecting World Heritage Sites, of which there are approximately 70 around the globe.

Lake Douglas is cupped in the Mark Range, above the Haast River as it flows to the sea. On a fine day, this north-westernmost corner of Mount Aspiring National Park affords a breathtaking view of the West Coast. But this is also where the rain falls big time. As clouds roll in from across the Tasman Sea, they hit the high wall of the Southern Alps and dump their heavy load in a torrent. Parts of the Coast receive up to seven metres of rain a year. By comparison, the drought-prone plains of central Otago, on the other side of the mountains, can expect a mere 500 millimetres of rain a year.

Tiny Lake Barra collects rainfall a thousand metres above the Haast River valley. The Haast Pass highway, between Wanaka and the West Coast, runs beside the river, following much the same route Maori travelled for centuries in search of greenstone, a highly valued variety of jade used to make ornaments and weapons. Construction was completed in 1965, and the pass named in honour of Austrian naturalist Julius von Haast, who spent many years exploring the area.

Otago

At 3027 metres high, Mt Aspiring is the highest peak in Otago. Rising from the icefields of four glaciers, and cutting a profile that invites comparison with the Matterhorn, it is an inspiration to climbers. Mt Aspiring National Park borders on Fiordland National Park to the south and is circumscribed by the Haast River to the north.

OTAGO

World-famous Milford Sound is the jewel in the Fiordland crown. It is presided over by the majestic Mitre Peak, which rises a dizzying one-and-a-half kilometres above the water. Thousands of tourists visit the 22-kilometre-long sound every year, taking one of the boat trips across its bottomless depths. Others tackle the Milford Track, often cited as the finest walk in the world. Rain is almost guaranteed in the sound — around eight metres falls every year. However, far from spoiling the experience, rain creates a magical landscape of cascading waterfalls, the grandest of which is the 508-metre Sutherland Falls.

An inlet on Lake Hawea nearly connects with Lake Wanaka. The isthmus between the lakes, known as the Neck, carries State Highway 6 on its way to the West Coast via Haast Pass. Lake Hawea is 410 metres deep, its bottom 64 metres below sea level. Its milky blue-green hue comes from finely ground rock particles borne by the glacial melt that feeds it. Land-locked salmon are common in the lake.

The Matukituki River empties into Lake Wanaka, north of Queenstown. A popular stop on the tourist trail, the town of Wanaka nevertheless maintains a more relaxed air than its frenetic neighbour. Equally scenic, and a good base for anyone visiting the Treble Cone and Cardrona ski-fields, it sells itself more on camping grounds and peaceful fishing than hotels and adventure thrills.

The Dart River, popular with jet-boaters, winds along the floor of a glacial valley beneath Mt Earnslaw. A New Zealand invention, the jet boat is extremely fast and highly manoeuvrable, and, with no propeller, can speed through shallows, even across a shingle bank, guaranteeing an exciting ride.

OTAGO

With two ninety-degree bends in its middle, Lake Wakatipu describes a distorted S. According to Maori legend the lake was created by a giant who, as he lay sleeping on his side, was burnt alive as punishment for kidnapping a beautiful girl. As the fire devoured him, the giant drew his knees up in agony, creating the distinctive shape. The name Wakatipu means 'the space of the giant'. The legend also offers an explanation for the lake's regular change in water level. Several times a day the water mysteriously rises and falls — to the rhythm of the giant's still beating heart.

Queenstown, on the shores of Lake Wakatipu, beneath the jagged Remarkables mountain range, is New Zealand's adventure capital. The town thrives on the business of providing thrills and spills for the hundreds of thousands of tourists who flock there each year to go bungy jumping, tandem parachuting, white-water rafting and jet-boating. Both Coronet Peak, up the valley behind the town, and the Remarkables range, closer to the lake, boast ski-fields with an international reputation.

A tangle of meanders and oxbow lakes, the Taieri River (*above*) wends its way across a glacial valley in north Otago. From its source in the Lammerlaw Range it flows north then south, meeting the sea down the coast from Dunedin. Although appealing from the air, the country in which the Taieri performs its gymnastics is bleak and windswept. New Zealand's lowest recorded temperature, -20°C, was recorded nearby.

The Tranz Scenic train (*opposite above*) winds through the Taieri Gorge on its way from Dunedin towards Queenstown. While New Zealand's rail network is not extensive, a journey by train is often more scenic than by car. Mountainous terrain, particularly in the South Island, means railway lines are often unable to take a direct route. Sometimes they don't reach their stated destination at all. Passengers taking the train to Queenstown have to disembark at Cromwell, some 60 kilometres short, and take a bus for the remainder of the journey.

For nearly a century Lake Mahinerangi (*opposite below*) has provided New Zealand with hydroelectric power. The artificial lake, one of several in the South Island, is formed by a dam on the Waipori River, inland from Dunedin. Lost to the rising waters when the dam was built was an abandoned gold-mining settlement on the banks of the river. About 75 percent of New Zealand's electricity consumption is fed by hydro-stations.

OTAGO

NEW ZEALAND FROM THE AIR

OTAGO

Dunedin, the South Island's second largest city, bears the Gaelic name of Scotland's capital city, Edinburgh. Its citizens are proud of their Scottish heritage, and even speak with a soft burr. Dunedin's university was the country's first, and provides the city with a sizeable student population. The long sandy beach at St Kilda offers swimmers the chance to brave heavy surf and sub-Antarctic temperatures.

Otago Harbour is the breached crater of a huge volcano. Ships dock at Port Chalmers, closer to the entrance than Dunedin, to which it is connected by road and rail. In 1882, the cargo vessel *Dunedin* sailed from the harbour with New Zealand's first shipment of frozen meat, launching what was to become a booming export industry, still New Zealand's largest earner, with markets in America, Europe, the Middle East and Japan. Taiaroa Head, overlooking the harbour entrance, is home to a colony of royal albatross — the closest in the world to human habitation.

The sculpted green hills of the Otago Peneplain, an area heavily eroded by ice millions of years ago, are classic sheep country. Until recently there were about 70 million sheep in New Zealand, although a tightening of the market has seen numbers decline to nearer 50 million — or 14 sheep to each person. New Zealand still provides 64 percent of the world's sheep meat and has the world's fourth largest flock.

As it nears the coast, the mighty Clutha River splits into two branches that snake their separate ways across a fertile alluvial plain. The land in between, the Inch Clutha, is effectively an island. The Clutha River drains Lakes Wanaka and Hawea in the Southern Alps. While 16 kilometres shorter than the North Island's Waikato River, it carries twice as much water. Clutha is the name Gaelic-speakers give the River Clyde, which runs through Glasgow, in Scotland.

NEW ZEALAND FROM THE AIR

The inviting beaches of Cannibal Bay, at the foot of the South Island's east coast, belie its grisly past. Warriors loyal to Tuhawaiki, one of the southern chiefs, failed in their attempt to ambush a scouting party of the North Island invader Te Rauparaha, and were slaughtered and eaten. The remaining bones were discovered by the early European settlers, who named the bay accordingly. According to Maori history, Tuhawaiki escaped the fate of his men by swimming 10 kilometres to Tuhawaiki Island, in Jack's Bay.

Southland

The South Fiord of Lake Te Anau penetrates the ranges on Fiordland's eastern edge. The Murchison Mountains, which rise to the north, were the scene of a sensational discovery in 1948, when ornithologist and hunter Geoffrey Orbell found takahe — a species of rail thought to have been extinct for more than 50 years — still living among the alpine tussock. Today the surviving birds are carefully monitored, and there is a captive breeding programme to increase numbers.

NEW ZEALAND FROM THE AIR

SOUTHLAND

Trampers on the Kepler Track (*previous*), in Fiordland National Park, generally take a break at the Forest Burn shelter near the Mt Luxmore saddle. The view of Lake Te Anau is typical of the endless vistas that make the Kepler one of New Zealand's great walks. Opened in 1988, the track is easily accessed from the town of Te Anau and follows 67 kilometres of mountain ridges and deep valleys. Being of only moderate difficulty, albeit with some steep ascents, it has become popular. It takes four or five days to complete, and there are comfortable huts along the way for spending the night.

The mountains around Jackson Peak loom above the Iris Burn (*above*) like a vertical wall. Fiordland National Park is New Zealand's largest national park, more than twice the size of Kahurangi and with over a million hectares of forest. Above the clearly visibly tree line, little survives the freezing winter conditions.

The Iris Burn trickles through beech forest close to the Kepler Track. Beech trees, hardy natives well suited to Fiordland's bitterly cold winters, make up the bulk of the forests in southwestern New Zealand. Only the tip of South America is closer to the Antarctic Circle than New Zealand; however, while Fiordland resembles the fjord-indented coast of Norway, it is closer to the equator. If Fiordland occupied the same position in the northern hemisphere as it does in the southern, it would be in the south of France.

Cradled between the serried ranks of mountains that stretch to the Fiordland horizon are many lakes, such as Lake Monowai, in the shadow of the Kaherekoau Mountains. Most of the lakes on the east side of the Southern Alps lie in hollows carved out by glaciers. Since the last ice age, the glaciers have been steadily retreating, their melt water collecting in the valleys they have vacated.

SOUTHLAND

The Makarewa River (*above*) winds through cattle pasture near Invercargill, New Zealand's southernmost city. Farming communities are scattered across the Southland Plains, for which Invercargill (*right*) serves as the main centre, their livestock grazing on the greenest grass in the country. Like Dunedin, Invercargill has a Scottish heritage, reflected in its many streets named after Scottish rivers and the distinctive burr in the local accent. Not only is Southland New Zealand's coldest province, it also has the least sunshine and the most rainy days.

The Oreti pub (*above*), standing at a lonely crossroads, exemplifies the way of life in the sparsely populated rural south. The plain around the Oreti River provides pasture for cattle and sheep. Working on the farm is often a solitary occupation, and a trip into town a rarity. For regular socialising, the scattered farming community meets in the pub for locally brewed beer and televised sport.

Stewart Island's few hundred residents live round Halfmoon Bay (*opposite above*). In the past, whalers, sealers, tin and gold miners and timber millers have all crossed the 30-kilometre-wide Foveaux Strait to make their fortune on Stewart Island, but today it is a quiet, secluded place visited mostly by tourists and nature lovers keen to walk some of the country's most rewarding tracks. Access is by ferry from Bluff or by air from Invercargill.

Maori know Stewart Island as Rakiura, 'land of the glowing skies'. Occasionally those skies flicker with the aurora australis — the southern lights — adding to the allure of an already magical place (*opposite below*). Heavily bushed and scarcely inhabited, the island has 1600 kilometres of coastline, deeply indented with inlets and coves. It remains one of New Zealand's outstanding wilderness areas.

SOUTHLAND

Lloyd Homer is one of New Zealand's leading landscape and panoramic photographers, specialising in aerial photography. In 1959 he joined the New Zealand Geological Survey, now part of the Institute of Geological and Nuclear Sciences. His photography has appeared in numerous publications. He lives in Upper Hutt, near Wellington.

John Gauldie is a freelance writer based in Seatoun, Wellington. Since completing a degree in journalism from the University of Hawaii, he has worked in Europe, Australia and New Zealand. He now divides his time between New Zealand and Europe.